DK Eye Wonder

Castle and knight

LONDON, NEW YORK, MUNICH,
MELBOURNE, and DELHI

Written and edited by Fleur Star
Designed by Jacqueline Gooden
and Laura Roberts

Publishing manager Susan Leonard
Managing art editor Clare Shedden
Jacket designer Bob Warner
Jacket editor Carrie Love
Jacket copywriter Adam Powley
Picture researcher Liz Moore
Production Luca Bazzoli
DTP Designer Almudena Díaz
Consultant Christopher Gravett

First published in Great Britain in 2006 by
Dorling Kindersley Limited
80 Strand, London WC2R ORL

A Penguin Company

2 4 6 8 10 9 7 5 3 1

ISBN 1-4053-0983-0

Colour reproduction by Colourscan, Singapore
Printed and bound in Italy by L.E.G.O.

Discover more at
www.dk.com

Contents

What is a castle?

There are hundreds of amazing castles all over the world. They were more than just homes for important people, such as kings and lords – they were also defence posts against enemies. The earliest castles were built more than 1,200 years ago. Some still stand today.

Forts first

Forts, such as this one in Mycenae, Greece, existed long before castles. Like castles, they were used for defence but, while an army could sleep there, they were never used as homes.

The crenellations at the top of a castle are sometimes called battlements.

Stone towers were much stronger than early wooden ones.

Most windows were small to stop attackers climbing through.

A typical castle?

Bodiam Castle, in southern England, was started in 1385. It has many defence features to stop enemy attackers, such as a very wide moat that was difficult to cross.

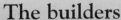

Tools used hundreds of years ago look much the same as those we use today.

Chisel

Dividers

Lump hammer

In the loop

Most castles have lots of loopholes that soldiers would shoot arrows through. The narrow slit made it harder for the enemy outside to shoot arrows back.

This French painting shows castle-building in the 1400s.

The builders

A lord needed permission from the king or ruler to build a castle. He would get a master mason to design and build the castle, which took many years and many teams of builders.

The small, tall tower was a lookout post.

Castle words

Castle a fortified home for a lord or king.

Crenellations the up-and-down stonework on top of the castle.

Master mason the person in charge of designing and building a castle.

5

Early castles

Castle building really got going in Europe in the 11th century. Some were simple, wooden buildings with a fence and ditch around them for protection. The next step up, motte and bailey castles, had a big advantage: height.

Wood or stone?

- Wooden castles were quick to build and repair...
- ...but they were easy to attack and burn down.
- Stone castles were stronger and did not rot like wood...
- ...but they were expensive and took many years to build.

The wooden fence, called a palisade, was later made of stone.

High sight

A motte was an important part of castle defence. By piling up earth and building the castle tower on top, people inside could see an attacking army coming a long way off.

A drawbridge could be raised to stop attackers climbing up to the motte.

The earth taken for the motte left a ditch, which was an extra defence.

When William the Conqueror invaded England in 1066,

From wood to stone

The earliest stone castle was built more than 1,000 years ago in northern France – before many wooden castles. Stone castles were not popular at first because they took more time and money to build.

Looks like a good spot

Castles were built in the best places to fight off the enemy. But often, the castle builders were not the first people to use the site. These ruins at Portchester Castle, England, lie within the remains of a Roman fort.

Low life

Down on the ground was the bailey, or courtyard, where animals were kept. Staff based here could run up the wooden bridge to the tower when the enemy came near.

A typical bailey would contain stables, a hall, workshops, and a chapel.

The bridge across the moat could be lifted to stop unwelcome visitors.

he built two wooden castles in two weeks!

A castle grows

In 1077, William the Conqueror started work on a stone keep by the River Thames in London, which became known as the Tower of London. More walls were added in the 13th century, and it has been changing ever since.

William the Conqueror ruled England from 1066.

The tower was the first thing seen when arriving in London by boat.

The White Tower
William's stone keep took more than 20 years to build. Once used as a residence, it became a store for weapons, jewels, and even prisoners!

The tower is 28 m (90 ft) high – three times as big as its neighbours in the Middle Ages.

Outer curtain wall

The inner curtain wall has twelve towers.

Murky moat

In 1275, King Edward I added a 50 m- (160 ft-) wide moat. It took six years to build but was drained in 1830 because the water was foul. Human bones were found at the bottom when it was emptied.

This area would have been filled with water.

The Tower in the year 1200. The walls behind and at the top right are the old Roman walls that once surrounded the city of London.

The outer curtain wall and the moat were both in place by 1300. It was now a concentric castle, because it had a double wall.

Today's Tower has many more buildings, including offices and barracks, but others, such as the Great Hall, have gone.

Who lived there?

During the later Middle Ages, from the 10th to the 16th centuries, kings and lords lived in castles. Their servants slept in the castle too, but the farming peasants lived in huts.

Ladies had female servants and nurses to bring up their children.

Lady of the manor
A lady would marry very young, usually around the age of 12. She gave all she owned to her husband.

Lord of the manor
As well as running his estate and being a judge, the lord's job was to be part of an army and go to war.

The apprentice
The squire was the lord's attendant, and trained to become a knight.

A new page
Noble-born sons were sent away to other castles to become pages.

The lady looked after important guests.

Lady

Lord

Squire

Page

Squires started training around the age of 13.

Lords grew rich from winning wars and tournaments.

A page became a squire when he grew up.

Chaplain's room

Upper hall

Chapel

Stair turret

Kitchen

Lower hall

Behind closed doors
Early castles were not pleasant to live in. The only heating in the large rooms came from open fires, so it was cold and draughty. Apart from the lord, only the chaplain was important enough to have his own bedroom.

Down on the farm
Most peasants worked in the lord's fields, growing food for the lord. He sold any spare crops to make money.

The peasants' huts were in the fields, and were owned by the lord.

Peasant

Spinster

Wool had to be spun so it could be used to make clothes.

Castle staff
The lord had lots of staff. Some were important officials, like the constable who looked after the castle when the lord was away. The more basic tasks were done by servants, such as cooks and weavers.

Carpenters made household objects and repaired the castle.

Carpenter

Food glorious food

The great hall was a castle's main room. Here the lord would eat, entertain guests, and do business. At first, the whole household slept in the hall, but by about the 13th century, the lord and his family had their own bedrooms.

A feast of fun

The lord's family would enjoy a large evening meal. When they had guests, there would be a full banquet, with jugglers and minstrels.

This is the Great Hall of Warwick Castle, England.

These three doors lead to the kitchens.

Only rooms on the upper storeys would have large windows.

Some floors were tiled. Carpets were rare and had to be imported.

In the kitchen

Large castles usually had more than one kitchen. Food was kept in a pantry and cooked in the kitchen. Drinks were stored in a buttery, which was named after the butts, or barrels, that stored drink.

Pigeon was often eaten, along with beef, pheasant, and venison.

All the food would be grown or caught on the lord's estates.

Cooking tools

While knives and spoons have not changed for centuries, some utensils are quite different today. Scary-looking flesh hooks were used to lift meat out of the pot, which was hung over a fire.

Cooking pot

Flesh hook

Sauces were used to cover up the taste of bad meat.

Dinner is served

The main meal was eaten in the late morning. Meat and fish were the central dishes. Dessert was a luxury. The food was eaten off bread "plates", called trenchers.

Drink it up

In the Middle Ages, water was so foul that you could not drink it. An alewife made ale for the staff. The lord and his guests were more important so they had wine, which was more expensive.

Time out

In the Middle Ages, there were no weekends! Peasants only had time off to go to church on Sundays, and fairs on feast days. But lords and ladies had plenty of time to relax.

Playing the fool

The job of a jester, or fool, was to make his lord laugh. He wore a silly costume with jingling bells, and told jokes.

The sound of music

Most people could not read, so listening to music was educational as well as fun. Minstrels sang songs about war, love, and religion.

Instruments of the time included pipes, trumpets, drums, and strings.

Lutes came to Europe from Arabia.

The entertainers

On a feast day or religious holy day, such as Easter, musicians and actors would tell the story of the festival at a village fair.

Time for prayers

Castles had their own chapels, which the lord, his family, and the castle staff had to attend daily. The lord employed a chaplain, who could read and taught lessons from the Bible.

What's the catch?

Hunting, especially with birds, was a daytime activity for the whole family. Anything caught would be eaten for supper.

Dicing with danger

Men used to play with dice as a gambling game. Some people enjoyed it so much, they lost fortunes.

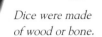

Dice were made of wood or bone.

Your move

Playing games was one way of passing long evenings. Chess, backgammon, and draughts were popular – and still are today.

Chess pieces represent the different classes in society, from the king down to pawns.

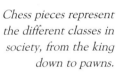

Bishop   *Knight*   *King*

Under siege

Living in a castle wasn't easy. Other lords wanted your land, and foreign invaders might need to capture your castle before they could conquer the country. There was a constant threat of being under siege.

PAT ON THE HEAD

It wasn't just arrows or starvation that killed a castle's inhabitants: the attackers lobbed dung into the castle to spread disease. They also threw the heads of captured soldiers, scaring those inside.

Sling

Dung

Large rock

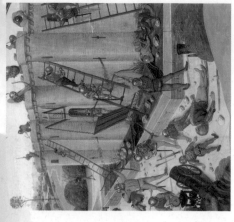

What is a siege?

The enemy would raid a village and surround its castle. They set up camp and waited... and waited... until either the lord surrendered, or he died of starvation inside. If things took too long, they attacked.

... and shoot!

This massive crossbow machine is called a ballista. It was aimed at people, and one of these outside the castle gates would stop defenders coming out.

The bolt shoots forward when the bow is released.

This shows where the bolt sits.

Whoosh Whoosh

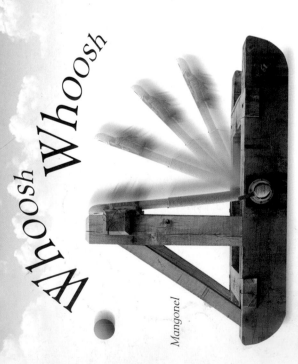

Mangonel

Ready, aim...

It was difficult to attack the high castle walls, but catapults such as the mangonel and trebuchet helped. They were used to fling rocks over the battlements.

16

Means of attack

As well as hand weapons and machines, the attackers used a variety of sneaky ways to get into the castle. These included climbing up drains and even bribing the guards!

Trebuchet

Not all sieges came to a bloody end: the lord would often surrender.

Arrowheads

The archers on the ground used different types of arrows in their longbows. A broadhead was used for killing animals, while a bodkin could pierce armour.

General purpose

Broadhead

Bodkin

Tricks of defence

The attack has started, and the enemy are at the gate. The small garrison, or army, inside the castle are up on the battlements. Can they stop the enemy from getting in?

Unwelcome visitors could end up trapped inside the gatehouse, below the murder holes.

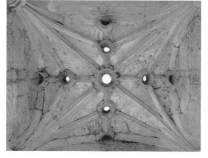

Up inside the top of the arch were the murder holes. Soldiers poured boiling liquid onto the enemy through these.

Shut the gate!

A gatehouse protected a castle's entrance. It usually had at least one heavy portcullis gate, which was lowered to cover the wooden doors behind. Some gatehouses had a defended area in front, which was called a barbican.

In hot water!

Contrary to popular belief, boiling oil was rarely used as a weapon, but boiling water and hot sand were often thrown over the battlements onto the enemy below.

However it lands, one spike always sticks up.

Watch your step

The garrison threw spiky metal caltrops on the ground, to injure the feet of enemy soldiers or horses who stood on them.

Hide out

Crenellations were made to hide behind. Soldiers took cover behind the higher walls, and peered out to shoot arrows over the lower parts.

Crenellations

Round and round...

Spiral staircases inside a castle usually turned to the right. This meant that an attacker going up had little room to swing his sword – but a defender coming down had plenty.

Soldiers dropped objects through these holes, called machicolations.

19

Lock 'em up

Castle towers were the ideal place to lock up prisoners, because they were strong buildings that were hard to break out of. Nobles who were captured in war were imprisoned so they could be held to ransom.

This collar weighs about 16 kg (35 lb). Heavy!

The collar locks around a person's neck.

No escape

Nobles held to ransom were kept in good conditions. Other prisoners were chained up as punishment, and to stop them escaping.

Behind bars

People caught misbehaving in the Middle Ages would usually face a fine or execution. Those "inside" were political or church prisoners or criminals awaiting trial.

The cuff would fit around a prisoner's ankle.

A royal pain

It was common to torture prisoners, sometimes with instruments. In England you had to get a licence from the king or queen to torture prisoners.

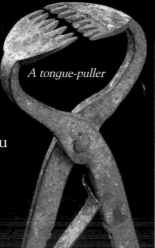

A tongue-puller

HISTORY MYSTERY

Edward V was just 12 years old when he became king in 1483. His uncle Richard locked him and his brother in the Tower of London, supposedly for their own protection. Richard then claimed the throne for himself, and the boys disappeared... 200 years later, workmen found bones in the tower. Had he murdered them?

Help, Help!

A long stretch

Many "confessions" were given under torture. Before the rack was invented, some prisoners were tied between two horses and pulled apart. Others were made to stand in burning hay.

Vaults would often have neck or leg chains secured to the posts.

Looks like someone's been locked up too long.

Where am I?

Not every castle had a prison. Those without would keep their prisoners in any spare room. In 1553, Bishop Latimer was kept in a hen house at the Tower of London!

The knight

Kings and dukes needed armies to defend their lands. It was the lord's job to serve his ruler by being a knight – a professional soldier who fought on horseback.

Plate armour was the knight's best defence against weapons.

It was important to protect the horse in battle.

A team of horses
A knight had to have is own armour and a horse. Some even had five horses: for war, hunting, jousting, travelling, and carrying baggage.

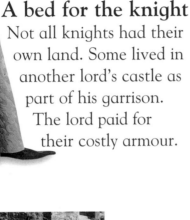

The lord

Women warriors

While only men could be knights, ladies were expected to defend their husband's castle. Some even went to war – including nuns!

In 1429, Joan of Arc tried to save the French king by leading an army into battle.

A bed for the knight

Not all knights had their own land. Some lived in another lord's castle as part of his garrison. The lord paid for their costly armour.

Samurai were famous for their archery skills with bows 2 m (6 ft) long.

Samurai were the ruling class of Japan until the 16th century.

Knight or not?

Japanese warriors were not knights, they were Samurai. They lived by their own rules called *bushido*, which means "the way of the warrior".

Follow the leader

A knight employed staff who followed him into battle. They helped him mount and dismount his horse, and looked after the horses and weapons.

Knight school

A lord had to go through training to become a knight. Work started early: around seven years old, a lord's son would leave home to work as a page. This led on to being a squire.

Are you being served?

Both pages and squires served the lord's family at dinner. Squires would do the more impressive jobs, such as carving meat. Pages might pour the drinks.

Practice makes perfect

Learning to ride horses and control weapons was vital. Aiming a lance at a target was a common way of training.

Even trained knights kept practising.

The wooden board swings round when it is hit.

No pain, no gain

A page became a squire about the age of 13. The lord then trained him to be a knight. He had to learn how to fight and use weapons, which included wrestling and throwing javelins. He would be dubbed, or made a knight, around the age of 21.

First lessons

A page was taught manners by the lady of the castle. Only some were taught to read.

Best behaviour

Knights had to behave in a certain way, which was called chivalry. It started out as rules for battle, but soon spread to everyday life.

Chivalry rules included how to treat ladies.

The lord wore an arming doublet under his armour.

It only took about 15 minutes to put on all the armour.

Dress to impress

The squire was the lord's personal servant. He dressed the lord in armour, looked after his weapons, and went everywhere with him – even into battle.

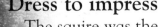

All wrapped up

The first thing that comes to mind when you think of a knight is his armour. No other horseback warriors in the world had armour that looked quite like the plate armour of the European knights.

Underarm protection

A besagew is more than a fancy plate: it provides extra defence by covering a chink. If they were left uncovered, weapons could get through these gaps.

Besagew

The couter does not bend, but you can move your arm inside it.

The gauntlet has a leather glove inside.

Chin up

The bevor protected the face and throat. The name comes from an Old French word that means "to dribble".

The average sword was 75 cm (30 in) long – as long as the knight's leg!

Symbolic sword

A knight's sword and spurs were given to him when he was dubbed. If these were taken away from him, it meant he was no longer a knight.

The knight used sharp spurs to control his horse.

The top of the cuisse, or thigh plate, straps on to the body.

The poleyn, or knee-covering, joins to the cuisse.

The greave over the shin is one of the first parts to put on.

The sabaton is made of a series of plates that move when you walk.

He's wearing a skirt!

There were no plates to cover the knight between the cuisse and the breastplate. Instead, he wore a skirt made of mail. It was flexible, so the knight could sit down.

Armour words

- **Chink** a gap in the armour where the plates meet.
- **Couter** a solid plate that covers the elbow.
- **Dubbing** the ceremony when a squire became a knight.
- **Mail** a kind of armour made of iron links.

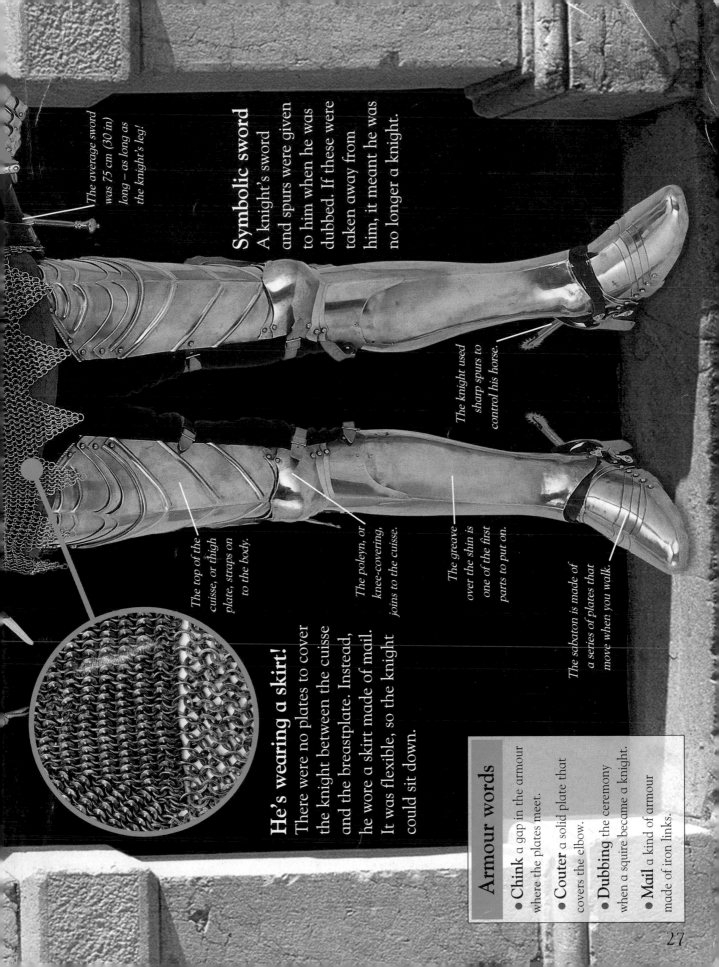

In shining armour

Soldiers have always needed protective clothing. The earliest types of armour were padded clothes and a mail jacket. Over time, weapons became stronger, and so did the armour.

Pollaxe

Armour basics

A suit of plate armour weighs 25 kg (55 lb), about the same as a seven year old child. It is made in sections, or plates, so it is quite easy to walk in, but it is very hot to wear.

Mail to plate

Mail is flexible armour made from iron rings linked together. It gave little protection against swords; hard steel plates were better.

Italian armour made in 1380.

Coming in the mail

The Bayeux Tapestry shows the Norman invasion of England in 1066. The knights are wearing mail suits and a coif, or hood made of mail, with a helmet on top.

On your head

During the 14th century, coifs were replaced by helmets with mail attached at the bottom. Many later helmets had no mail.

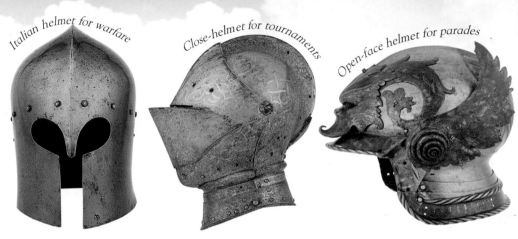

Italian helmet for warfare

Close-helmet for tournaments

Open-face helmet for parades

The height of fashion

Later armour, especially that used for parades and tournaments, was based on local fashions. It could take six men to make just one suit.

German armour made in 1500.

English armour made in 1587.

HEAVY KNIGHTS

It's a myth that armour was so heavy the knight had to be lifted onto his horse with a crane. But he did need attendants to pick him up if he fell off in battle and was hurt. They also cleaned his armour to stop it getting rusty – using a mixture of sand and their own urine.

Weapons of war

A knight was called on to fight battles about land ownership and who was ruler. It was not common to have large wars during the Middle Ages: a ruler could lose a whole army this way.

Mane protection

Warhorses were so valuable in battle that some were given armour. The most popular kind was a caparison, a cloth "skirt".

Soldiers had to follow rules of how to act in battle.

War hammer

Glaive

Mace

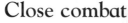

Close combat

Many weapons were mounted on long wooden staffs, or poles. Maces were shorter, which shows how closely the two sides fought.

Length of service

One of the few major wars of the Middle Ages was between France and England. It was called the Hundred Years' War, but it lasted 116 years, from 1337 to 1453!

Into battle

Knights made up only a part of an army. Foot soldiers protected them before they charged. During the 14th century, many knights dismounted and fought alongside the foot soldiers.

The army charged with staff weapons until they were near enough to use a mace or sword.

Joust for fun

The knights of the Middle Ages were more than soldiers – they were also the sports stars of the time! When not in battle, they entertained crowds with tournaments, which were also good practice for fighting.

Horseplay

Early tournaments had one event: a fight between teams of knights on horses. Other events were added later, so this one was renamed the tourney.

This knight has just broken his lance, so he has lost the joust.

How to play

Jousting was a high-speed skill. A knight had to knock his opponent off their horse using a lance. The victor could win lots of prize money.

The tilt, or fence, stops the horses charging into each other.

A lance would fit neatly into this gap.

On the defence

Each knight had his own shield to use in combat. This one was used during the joust – its curved edge supported a lance. The shield was important for defence.

Not playing fair

- In early times, many knights would be killed at tournaments.
- King Edward I banned tournaments because the knights were jousting instead of going to battle for him.

The handle was solid wood, for balance.

Lance

Lances for jousting were hollowed so they were not too heavy.

Choose your weapon

Early tournaments used sharp battle weapons. Later on, most weapons were blunted so the knights were not killed – but they could still be injured.

The mace could seriously damage armour.

Mace

When upright, the axe is as tall as an adult.

Pollaxe

Tournaments could have three events: the tourney, jousting, and foot combat.

Helmets were padded inside to protect the head.

Foot combat

Early foot tournaments saw two knights battling each other. This changed to whole teams fighting across a barrier. Prizes for these events were smaller.

Heraldry

Noble families each had a "coat of arms" – their own special symbol that was like having their own logo. Knowing who someone is from their coat of arms is called heraldry.

Early signs
One of the first coats of arms is shown on the tomb of Geoffrey Plantagenet, which dates back to 1160.

Geoffrey was Duke of Normandy, an important French nobleman.

Shield
When a knight was dressed in armour, it was hard to see who he was. So knights displayed their family coats of arms on their shields.

The pommel, or end of the sword, is shaped like a lion's head.

Presenting arms

- A knight would only ever have one coat of arms.

- Arms were passed down from father to son. If there was more than one son, the others would change the symbols.

- Arms are unique: no other person would have the same.

These are the arms of Cosimo de' Medici.

Every new coat of arms had to be registered.

Just for show
This sword belonged to the 16th-century Italian nobleman Cosimo de' Medici, the Duke of Florence. His arms show that he belonged to an order of knights.

Gules (red)

A lion means a generous spirit, and red is the colour of a warrior.

A dog means loyalty, and a silver background is peace.

What does it mean?

Heraldry has its own language, based on Old French, to describe the colours and patterns on arms. There is also a secret meaning behind the background colour and symbols used.

If arms are quartered, it shows two families that have joined together in marriage.

Vert (green)

A unicorn shows courage and purity, and green is hope and joy.

An owl means vigilance and wit, and a blue background is truth.

Azure (blue)

Argent (silver)

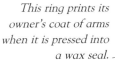

This ring prints its owner's coat of arms when it is pressed into a wax seal.

This pottery jar dates from around 1500.

A good impression

Arms were originally a status symbol of upper class families. But after knights displayed them, the rest of society caught on. Even towns would have their own arms.

35

The Crusades

In 1096, Christian Europeans went to the Middle East to fight the Saracens – Muslim warriors who were taking over the land. The nine wars that followed over the next 200 years were known as the Crusades.

How it began

The Christian Emperor of Byzantium asked Pope Urban II to help defend against the Saracens. He gave a speech to the rulers of Europe, and persuaded them to go to war.

The People's Crusade

It wasn't only knights who supported the Pope. Peasants, women, and children went off on their own People's Crusade. They were unsuccessful, but the knights reclaimed Jerusalem in the First Crusade – for a while.

This 16th-century picture of the Crusades shows the knights in 16th-century armour.

What's in a name?

- "Saracen" was the European name for all Muslims. Muslims called the Europeans "Franks".

- Alexius I was emperor of Byzantium, where Greece and Turkey are today.

As well as hospitals, the Knights of St John also built castles. The biggest is Krak des Chevaliers in Syria.

Order, order

Many Crusader knights signed up to military orders. The two most famous are the Knights Templar and the Knights of St John, who were also called the Knights Hospitaller because they looked after the sick.

This is the seal of the Knights Templar. The motto reads "The Seal of the Order of Christ".

The other side

The Crusaders fought against the Saracens, who fought on horseback, used curved swords, and carried round shields.

Following orders

After the Crusades, kings created their own orders so that knights would be loyal to them. By the 16th century, there were lots of new orders, including the Order of the Garter, whose symbol is a cross of St George.

Shopping trip

Europeans travelling to the Middle East saw a different world. They brought back exotic fruit, cotton clothes, and even sugar – before the 12th century, they used honey instead.

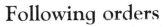

Sugar

Cotton

Dates

Moorish castles

The Moors were Arabs who came to Europe from north Africa. They brought with them a different type of castle design, with domes, arches, decorative walls, and water features.

Moor information

- The Moors ruled over large parts of Spain and Portugal in the Middle Ages.

- In 1492, the Catholic rulers of northern Spain drove the Moors out of southern Spain.

- The Spanish rulers captured the Alhambra, and lived there.

The four towers are called Square, Round, Tribute, and Crumb.

The castle by the river

The Almodóvar del Rio, in Córdoba, Spain, has a network of underground tunnels, dungeons, and water wells. It was important to have a store of water in case of a siege.

No one knows for sure how old this kasbah is, but it was probably built in the 16th century.

Film star

One of the most famous Arab castles, called kasbahs, is found in Ait Benhaddou in Morocco. Its style is so typical that it has featured in many Hollywood films.

Writing on the wall

Walls and ceilings inside Moorish castles are decorated in an Arabic style. They feature patterns of brightly-coloured tiles and verses from the Koran, the Islamic holy book.

Al-hamra means "the red one" – its walls glow red at sunset.

This door is in one of the Alhambra's royal palaces, where Moorish kings lived.

This part of a royal palace is called the Tower of Hens.

Enemies could be seen through the small gaps in the fort wall.

Fantastic feat

It took more than 140 years, from 1298, to build the Alhambra, in Granada, Spain. The oldest part is the fort, to which three royal palaces and an estate of cottages and gardens were added.

Asian castles

With their own unique styles, Japanese, Chinese, and Indian castles are not only different to those in Europe, but also from one another.

A truly ancient castle

Yumbulagang castle was built in the 1st century BC. Its Tibetan name means "the palace of mother and son", because it has two parts.

The Sun's castle

Mehrangarh, in India, takes its name from *Mehr*, which means "Sun". Its walls are 37 m (120 ft) high and 6 m (20 ft) thick. No wonder it has never been captured!

Passage turrets connect the large tower to the three smaller ones.

Chinese emperors lived here from 1420 to 1911.

Castle city

China's Imperial Palace, in Beijing, is actually a whole fortified city, which was finished in 1420. It was also called "The Forbidden City" because commoners were not allowed to enter.

Himeji castle

Japan's biggest castle, Himeji, was first built as a fort in 1346 and has been rebuilt twice. Started in 1601, it took 50 million people nine years to build the tower!

The five-storey tower actually has seven levels inside.

A cool coat

Although the tower is stone, its frame and interior are wood. The outside is covered in plaster to make it fireproof.

Himeji is also called "White Heron Castle" because of its white walls.

Towering strengths

With their massive height and thick walls, towers are a castle's key defence. Although they were harder to build, round towers were better than square towers – but towers come in all shapes and sizes.

French

The Loire Valley, France, is famous for its castles, or châteaux. They have a special French design of narrow towers with high roofs.

The chapel is inside one of the two outer towers.

Chateau de Chambord is the Loire's largest castle.

The unusually-shaped towers are called "pepperpots".

There are four towers around the castle's keep.

A plan of the castle from above.

I like your style

Different castle styles depend on when and where they were built. Twelfth-century Gothic castles are tall and imposing, but 15th-century Renaissance castles are more ornate.

German Gothic

Some German castles, such as the Gothic-style Burg Eltz, have strange shapes. Built on mountains or crags, they had to fit the smallest of spaces.

Welsh walls

Conwy Castle in Wales is built into the town walls. The castle has eight round towers, and there are another 13 in the town walls. They are over 20 m (70 ft) tall.

Pieces of eight

The unique Castel del Monte in Italy has octagonal towers around an eight-sided keep. It was built by Frederick II in 1249 as a hunting lodge.

Swedish style

The town of Kalmar, Sweden, grew up around its 12th-century castle. The castle was rebuilt in 1540 in the Renaissance style, with decorative towers.

Castles today

Imagine living in a castle. In the Middle Ages they were cold and uncomfortable places to live. Later castles were grander, with more luxuries. Even now people build houses to look like castles as a sign of power and wealth.

The house on the hill

Casa Loma, or "the house on the hill", was built by Sir Henry Pellant between 1911 and 1914 in Toronto, Canada. But Sir Henry could not afford to pay for it, so he ended up living on a farm.

American dream

Between 1919 and 1947, in California, USA, William Randolph Hearst built himself a castle... and three guest houses, a zoo, swimming pools, and tennis courts!

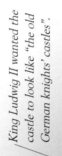

King Ludwig II wanted the castle to look like "the old German knights' castles".

Bed and board

If you want to live in a castle, you could stay in one on holiday. Some old castles are now hotels, and some new hotels look like romantic old castles.

This South African hotel is based on Castle Lichtenstein, which is in Germany.

It's a fairy tale

Walt Disney used Neuschwanstein as a model for Cinderella's castle in Walt Disney World, Florida.

Fit for a king

King Ludwig II wanted Neuschwanstein Castle to be his dream home. Work started in 1869. It was so ornate, it took 14 carpenters four years to do the carvings in his bedroom alone!

Glossary

Here are the meanings of some words that are useful to know when learning about castles and knights.

arming doublet A jacket worn under armour with mail attached to fill the gaps in the plates.

bailey The courtyard of a castle, which had workshops or other buildings inside. Animals were also kept here.

ballista A giant crossbow on wheels that shot massive bolts.

barbican Part of the defences on the outside of the castle walls. It usually protected the gate.

battlements The stonework on top of a castle with gaps for soldiers to shoot weapons through. Also called crenellations.

besagew The part of a suit of plate armour that covered the armpit.

bevor The part of a suit of plate armour that covered the neck and chin.

caltrop A four-pointed, spiked weapon thrown on the ground to injure horses and foot soldiers.

chaplain The man who led prayers in the chapel and taught lessons from the Bible to the family.

chivalry The knights' code of conduct – how they should behave in war and in love.

coif An early type of mail armour that covered the head.

concentric castle A castle with two walls around the outside.

couter The part of a suit of plate armour that covered the elbow.

crenellations Another name for battlements on top of a castle.

crossbow A bow with a wooden handle that shot short arrows called bolts.

cuisse The part of a suit of plate armour that covered the thigh.

dubbing The ceremony where a squire became a knight. He was tapped on the neck or shoulder with a sword.

feudal system The class system of the early Middle Ages in Europe. The king was at the top and owned all the land. Bishops and barons were below him, then the lesser lords, and finally the peasants. Feudalism died out by the 1600s.

fort A strong building or set of buildings that protected defenders. People did not live in a fort.

garrison A group of soldiers who lived in the castle.

gauntlet The part of a suit of plate armour that covered the hand, like a metal glove.

glaive A weapon with a long blade on the end of a pole.

great tower The main tower of a castle. It usually contained a hall, the lord's rooms, and store rooms.

greave The part of a suit of plate armour that covered the shin.

heraldry Using of coats of arms to identify knights and noble families.

joust A competition between two knights on horseback. They used lances to knock their opponent off his horse.

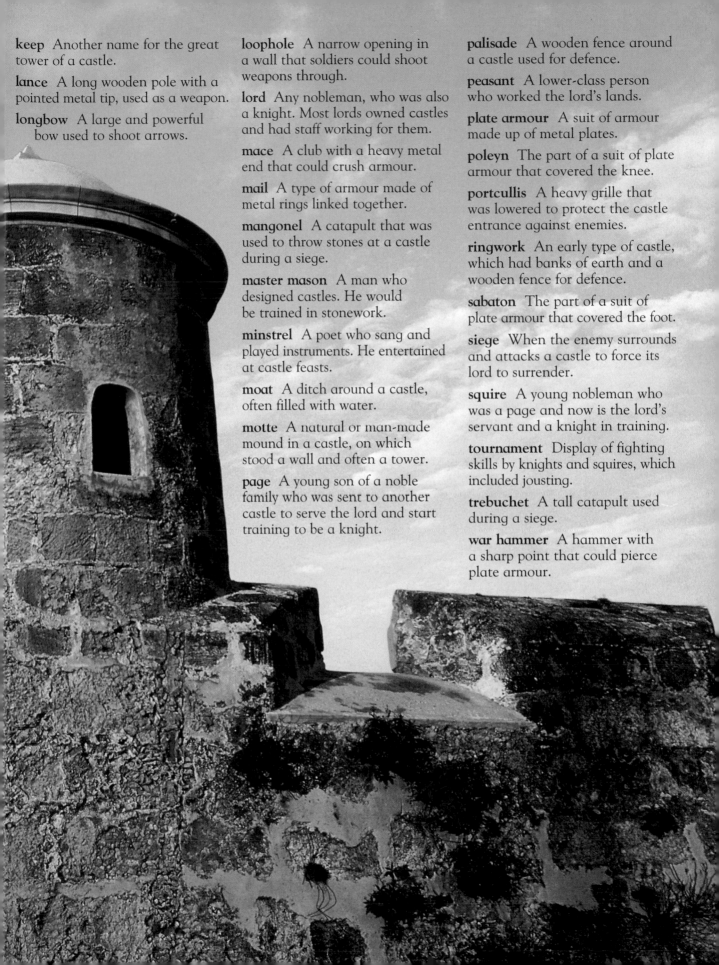

keep Another name for the great tower of a castle.

lance A long wooden pole with a pointed metal tip, used as a weapon.

longbow A large and powerful bow used to shoot arrows.

loophole A narrow opening in a wall that soldiers could shoot weapons through.

lord Any nobleman, who was also a knight. Most lords owned castles and had staff working for them.

mace A club with a heavy metal end that could crush armour.

mail A type of armour made of metal rings linked together.

mangonel A catapult that was used to throw stones at a castle during a siege.

master mason A man who designed castles. He would be trained in stonework.

minstrel A poet who sang and played instruments. He entertained at castle feasts.

moat A ditch around a castle, often filled with water.

motte A natural or man-made mound in a castle, on which stood a wall and often a tower.

page A young son of a noble family who was sent to another castle to serve the lord and start training to be a knight.

palisade A wooden fence around a castle used for defence.

peasant A lower-class person who worked the lord's lands.

plate armour A suit of armour made up of metal plates.

poleyn The part of a suit of plate armour that covered the knee.

portcullis A heavy grille that was lowered to protect the castle entrance against enemies.

ringwork An early type of castle, which had banks of earth and a wooden fence for defence.

sabaton The part of a suit of plate armour that covered the foot.

siege When the enemy surrounds and attacks a castle to force its lord to surrender.

squire A young nobleman who was a page and now is the lord's servant and a knight in training.

tournament Display of fighting skills by knights and squires, which included jousting.

trebuchet A tall catapult used during a siege.

war hammer A hammer with a sharp point that could pierce plate armour.

Index

Acknowledgements

Dorling Kindersley would like to thank:
Cathy Chesson for design assistance; Andy Cooke for artwork;
Peter Bull for digital artwork; Sarah Mills and Karl Stange
for picture library services.

Picture credits

The publisher would like to thank the following for their kind
permission to reproduce their photographs:
t-top, b-bottom, r-right, l-left, c-centre, a-above, f-far

1 Alamy Images: Alasdair Ogilvie/The National Trust Photolibrary. 2 DK
Images: Geoff Dann/Courtesy of the Wallace Collection, London tl. 3 Getty
Images: Photographer's Choice. 4 Corbis: Buddy Mays tl. 4-5 Alamy Images:
Worley Design. 5 Arcangel Images: tl. 5 www.bridgeman.co.uk:
Giraudon/Bibliotheque Sainte-Genevieve, Paris ca. 5 DK Images: Geoff
Dann/Courtesy of the National Guild of Stone Masons and Carvers, London tr,
tcl; Torla Evans/The Museum of London tc. 6-7 DK Images: Dave
Rudkin/Gordon Models - modelmaker. 7 Corbis: Robert Estall tr. 7 Photo-
Links.com: cla. 8 Corbis: Bettmann tl. 8 Getty Images: Robert Harding World
Imagery bl. 8-9 Topfoto.co.uk: HIP/English Heritage. 9 Alamy Images: Adrian
Chinery tr. 9 The Board of Trustees of the Armouries.
Ivan Lapper cra, crb, br. 10 Alamy Images: Liquid-Light Photography l. 10
Topfoto.co.uk: The British Library/HIP tl. 11 Alamy Images: geogphotos tl. 11
DK Images: Geoff Brightling/Courtesy of the Order of the Black Prince cb. 12
DK Images: British Library tl. 13 Corbis: Ludovic Maisant cal. 13 DK Images:
Torla Evans/The Museum of London bc, cbr. 14 Bodleian Library, University
of Oxford: tcr. 14 DK Images: Geoff Dann/Courtesy of the Anthony Barton
Collection c, bl. 14-15 A1 Pix: Superbild. 15 Collections: Roy Stedall-
Humphreys tl. 15 DK Images: Geoff Dann/The British Museum br, bcr, brl;
Torla Evans/The Museum of London c. 16 DK Images:

Colin Keates/Courtesy of the Natural History Museum, London ca. 16 The Picture
Desk: The Art Archive/JFB r. 16-17 Dick Clark. 17 Dick Clark: r. 18 Alamy Images:
Kevin White t. 19 Alamy Images: Seymour Rogansky b. 19 DK Images: Geoff
Dann/Courtesy of the Board of Trustees of the Royal Armouries cal. 19 Topfoto.co.uk:
HIP/The British Library tl. 20 Corbis: Richard T. Nowitz cra. 21 Chateau Chillon. 21
Corbis: Bettmann tl. 21 DK Images: Harry Taylor/Courtesy of the Natural History
Museum, London br. 22 Dick Clark: 23. akg-images: tc. 23 Dick Clark: clb. 23
Topfoto.co.uk: br. 24 www.bridgeman.co.uk: British Library tl. 24-25 Dick Clark. 25
DK Images: The British Museum cl. 25 The Picture Desk: The Art Archive tcl. 26-27
Corbis: Elio Ciol. 28 Dick Clark: l. 29 www.bridgeman.co.uk: Musee de la Tapisserie,
Bayeux, France with special authorisation of the city of Bayeux tcl. 29 Corbis:
Philidelphia Museum of Art bl. 29 DK Images: Geoff Dann/Courtesy of the Wallace
Collection, London cra, bc, cal, car. 30 Corbis: Kit Houghton tl. 30 DK Images: Geoff
Dann/The British Museum bcl. 30-31 Dick Clark. 31 www.bridgeman.co.uk: Earl of
Leicester, Holkham Hall, Norfolk tl. 32 Dick Clark: tl. 32-33 Dick Clark. 33 Dick
Clark: br. 33 DK Images: Geoff Dann/Courtesy of the Wallace Collection, London tl,
a, car. 34 DK Images: Geoff Dann/Courtesy of the Wallace Collection, London bc. 36
Corbis: Archivo Iconografico, SA tl, b. 37 Alamy Images: Expuesto/Nicolas Randall tr.
37 www.bridgeman.co.uk: Giraudon/Bibliotheque Nationale, Paris, France bl. 37
Corbis: Francis G. Mayer c; Origlia Franco/Sygma cra. 37 DK Images: Angus McBride
cla. 38 Alamy Images: LifeFile Photos Ltd/Emma Lee car; Pat Behnke bl. 38-39 Corbis:
Hubert Stadler. 39 Corbis: Ian Dagnall br. 40 Corbis: Patrick Ward tc. 40 A1
Pix: Superbild cra. 40 Alamy Images: Panorama Stock Photos Co Ltd/Hu Weibiao clb.
40 Corbis: Sheldan Collins cla. 40-41 Alamy Images: SC Photos/Dallas and John
Heaton. 41 Corbis: Michael S. Yamashita tr. 42-43 Alamy Images: AM Corporation.
43 Corbis: Dave Bartruff bc; Massimo Listri cb; Paul Thompson/Eye Ubiquitous ca. 43
Getty Images: Stone/Stephen Studd tc. 44 A1 Pix: tl. 44 Corbis: ChromoSohm
Inc./Joseph Sohm tr; Jose Fuste Raga bcr. 44-45 Getty Images: Taxi/Josef Beck. 45
Alamy Images: Ian Dagnall tl. 46-47 Getty Images: Image Bank/Angelo Cavalli. 48
Alamy Images: Trevor Smithers. 48 DK Images: Geoff Dann/Courtesy of The
Wallace Collection, London c.

All other images © Dorling Kindersley.

For further information see: www.dkimages.com